TRADITIONAL TALES
from

CHINA

Vic Parker

Based on myths and legends retold by
Philip Ardagh

Illustrated by
Micheal Fisher

Thameside Press

U.S. publication copyright © 2001 Thameside Press.

International copyright reserved in all countries.
No part of this book may be reproduced in any form
without written permission from the publisher.

Distributed in the United States by
Smart Apple Media
1980 Lookout Drive
North Mankato, MN 56003

Editor: Stephanie Turnbull
Designer: Zoë Quayle
Educational consultant: Margaret Bellwood

Library of Congress Cataloging-in-Publication Data

Parker, Vic.
    China / written by Vic Parker.
      p. cm. -- (Traditional tales from around the world)
    Summary: A collection of tales from China, including creation myths,
tales of gods and monsters, and the adventures of Monkey.
    ISBN 1-930643-37-3
    1. Tales--China. [1. Folklore--China.] I. Title.

PZ8.1.P2234 Ch 2001
398.2'0951--dc21

                        2001023215

Printed in Hong Kong

9 8 7 6 5 4 3 2 1

CONTENTS

CHINESE TALES

China is a huge country. It is as big as all the countries in Europe put together. The people who live in China make up a quarter of all the people in the world.

People have lived in China for thousands and thousands of years, but the country has always been cut off from the rest of the world. On one side is the wide Pacific Ocean. On all the other sides are enormous mountain ranges. One of them, the Himalayas, is the tallest, most dangerous mountain range in the world. Next to these mountains lie high, windswept plains and wide deserts.

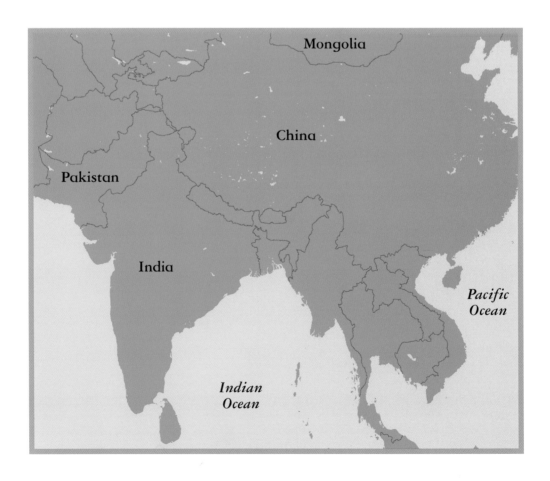

Today, China is ruled by a government that follows Communist ideas. This means that there is no emperor, no official religion, and all land and property is owned by the government.

Things were very different in the past. For thousands of years China was ruled by a series of powerful, wealthy emperors. The earliest Chinese people worshiped these emperors as gods.

Later, a wise man called Confucius taught spiritual ideas about peace. A holy man called Lao Zi developed a way of life called Taoism, which aimed to help people live simply and honestly. Buddhism also spread to China from India. Buddhists believe that by living a strict life they can find peace forever.

Many stories from these beliefs are still popular in China today. You can read new versions of some of these magical tales in this book.

This wooden carving shows one of the Eight Immortals, a group of ancient Chinese heroes. You can read a story about one of the Immortals on page 31.

THE THUNDER GOD'S GIFT

The farmer shook his fist angrily at the thick, black rain clouds. They had covered the skies for days.

"I've had enough, Thunder God!" the farmer exploded. "You've sent so many storms that my plants have stopped growing and the soil has been washed away."

The farmer pushed his daughter and son inside his house and hung a huge, iron cage from the roof.

"Come and fight me!" he screamed.

In Heaven, the mighty Thunder God thought he heard someone squeaking his name. He grabbed his enormous battle-ax and swooped down to Earth to see what was going on. Quick as a flash, the farmer speared the Thunder God with a long iron fork, thrust him into the cage and slammed the door.

"Got you!" the farmer crowed triumphantly.

The Thunder God spent a miserable night in his new prison. Next morning, the clouds had cleared and the rains were gone. The god was defeated and the farmer was delighted.

"I'm going to buy some herbs," he told his two children.

"I'm going to use them to pickle the Thunder God and put him on display! Now, don't talk to him, don't touch him, and most of all, DON'T give him a drink."

As soon as the farmer had gone, his little daughter and son crept outside to peek at the Thunder God. How sad he looked! The children kept at a safe distance and watched. The Thunder God didn't seem to have any magic or strength left. Hour after hour, he just crouched there, looking miserable.

At noon the little girl suggested, "Let's have a drink and then we'll go and play."

As the children stood under a shady tree and sipped some refreshing water, the Thunder God turned and looked at them with huge, sad eyes.

"Have mercy," he whispered. "It is so hot here in the blazing sun. I am dying of thirst. Please give me a drink."

"We're not allowed to," replied the little girl, realizing too late that she had broken one of her father's orders.

"I promise I will not harm you," the Thunder God moaned. "A god cannot break his word. Now I beg you, give me a drink."

The children couldn't help feeling sorry for him. Trembling, the little girl handed a spoonful of water through the bars.

The farmer hadn't told his children that the Thunder God drew all his power from water. At the first drop, new strength flooded into his body. With a great roar, he broke out of the iron cage as easily as if the bars were made of straw.

"Thank you!" the Thunder God boomed. "I would like you to have this gift in return for your kindness."

He pulled a tooth from his mouth and threw it on the ground. "From now on, your names will be Gourd Girl and Gourd Boy. Use my gift wisely." With that, the Thunder God vanished into the sky in a flash of light.

Before the children's eyes, a tiny green shoot sprang up from the tooth. It swelled into a juicy, round vegetable called a gourd. The gourd grew and grew until it was bigger than the children. By the time the gourd stopped growing, the skies had darkened once again.

As enormous drops of rain began to splash down, the farmer returned home.

"You stupid children!" he raged. "The Thunder God is going to punish me by sending a huge flood! We're all going to drown!"

The children shuddered as an ear-splitting clap of thunder rang out. Waterfalls of rain poured from the heavens. Streams of water gushed over the ground.

Over the noise of the storm, the children suddenly heard the clanging of metal. Their father had begun to build an iron boat to escape the flood. The astonished girl and boy suddenly remembered the Thunder God's words: *Use my gift wisely*. At once, they realized what they had to do....

The children hurriedly cracked open the giant gourd. They scooped out the fleshy insides, making the gourd into a hollow, light boat. By this time the swirling waters were up to their chests. They jumped aboard just in time before the boat was swept away. Their father was already afloat—and still the waters were rising.

The flood carried the two little boats up and up and up . . . until the water reached the gates of Heaven itself.

"Help!" yelled the farmer, banging on the gates.

The Lord of Heaven heard the commotion and realized what was happening.

"Quick!" he ordered the Thunder God. "Your flood is going to destroy the Kingdom of Heaven! Get rid of all this water at once!"

The Thunder God did as he was ordered. One minute, the whole world was water. Next second, it was all gone.

"Aaaaaarghhh!" cried the farmer and his children as the two boats dropped through the empty skies.

CRASH! The iron boat hit the ground and smashed into a million pieces. SPLAT! The farmer came to a messy end.

THUD! The soft gourd boat bounced on the ground and rolled gently to a halt. The two children tumbled out with nothing more than a few bruises.

Gourd Girl and Gourd Boy found they were the only people left alive on the whole Earth. With Heaven's help, the wise sister and brother created a whole new race of people. They scattered pieces of flesh into the wind and each one that fell on land became a new human being. As for Gourd Girl and Gourd Boy, they became gods and today they watch over the Earth from Heaven.

THE STORY OF THE SUNS

The god and goddess of the eastern sky had ten very special children. They were burning suns that glowed with warmth and light. The ten suns lived far beyond the eastern sea, in the branches of a giant mulberry bush that reached up into the heavens.

Every day, one sun walked across the sky, bringing life to the world below. Only one sun went out at a time. The ten children never walked together, because their mother had strictly forbidden it.

After a thousand years, the suns began to get bored.

"Why can't we go out and play with each other?" complained one.

"It would be so much fun to chase each other across the sky!" said a second.

"I wonder why Mother will not let us," sighed a third.

"Maybe she is worried that we will misbehave," suggested a fourth.

"Or that one of us will get lost," added a fifth.

"Perhaps if we showed Mother that we can be good and responsible, she would change her mind," said a sixth.

13

"Yes!" gasped an eighth. "We could creep out early, before Mother notices, and surprise her!"

"What a great idea!" laughed the ninth sun.

"We'll do it tomorrow," agreed the tenth sun.

Next morning, before the goddess of the eastern sky was awake, the ten suns dashed excitedly across the heavens, laughing and dancing and playing tag. It was even more fun than they had imagined!

The suns were so carried away that they didn't once look down at the Earth. Far below them, terrible things were happening. Ten suns meant ten times the brightness and heat. People were blinded by the blazing light. Birds were scorched. Gasping animals were dying. Crops burst into flame. Forests turned brown and dusty. Rivers and lakes disappeared, leaving fish choking. Even huge seas began to dry up.

When the god and goddess of the eastern sky saw what was going on, they were horrified. They ordered their ten children to return home, but the suns disobeyed them. They were having too much fun! The god and goddess tried begging and pleading, but it was no use. The joyful suns ignored them!

Down below on Earth, the people were dying from the terrible heat. Their ruler, an emperor, was desperate.

Each day, he spent long hours praying to the god and goddess for help. The emperor was a good and kind leader, so the god and goddess took pity on him. They commanded their archer, Yi, to hurry to him at once.

Yi had ten magical arrows in his quiver—one for each sun. He put an arrow to his bowstring, fired, and a sun exploded in the sky. Its spirit fell to Earth in the form of a three-legged raven. Yi then shot the second, third, fourth, and fifth sun.... At first the emperor was delighted, but as Yi shot the sixth and seventh suns, a terrible thought crossed his mind. What if the archer shot all the suns? Then the Earth would be cold and dark. It would be just as dangerous as the Earth being burning and bright.

While Yi took aim at the eighth sun, the wise emperor quietly slid an arrow from the quiver and hid it in his robe. When Yi had shot the ninth sun, he found he had no arrows left. His job was done—and there was still one sun left in the sky.

While the emperor and his people rejoiced on Earth, the god and goddess of the eastern sky were heartbroken.

"You have done your job well, Yi," they told the archer sadly. "But we can no longer bear to look at you. Each time we see you, we will be reminded of our nine dead children. You and your wife must leave Heaven forever!"

Yi's wife, Heng E, was furious at having to live with humans. She hated her new home on Earth, and every day she sat sulking indoors. Yi, on the other hand, went out exploring new places and meeting new people. Gradually, he started to spend more and more time away from home. Heng E grew curious about what her husband was up to. One day, while Yi was out, Heng E searched the house for clues.

High in the rafters, Heng E found a small, glowing package. She unwrapped it with trembling fingers. It was a little tablet! Heng E wondered what kind of pill this was.

The tablet was in fact a pill of everlasting life. On one of Yi's trips, he had built an amazing palace for a goddess. The delighted goddess had given Yi the wonderful tablet as a thank-you gift. It was too powerful for just one person and was meant for both Yi and his wife to share, so that they could both live forever. Yi had hidden the tablet to keep it safe.

Heng E knew none of this. She was dying to find out what the tablet was. She put it on her tongue to have a little taste.

At that very moment, Yi returned home.

Gulp! Heng E swallowed the pill.

We will never know whether she did this deliberately
or by accident, but we know for sure what happened next.
Heng E had swallowed a strong pill made for two people!
Immediately, her body began to fade and shimmer.
She floated out of the door and away up into the sky.

Up, up, up went Heng E, until she reached the moon,
where she lives to this day.

In spite of what Heng E had done, Yi loved his wife
very much. He built a palace on the one remaining sun,
so he could be near her. You can tell when Yi visits her,
because on those nights the moon shines brightest.

THE YEAR
OF THE DOG

There was once an emperor who was one of the richest men in the whole world. He had a huge kingdom and ruled over millions of people. He had an enormous palace, filled with priceless furniture and works of art. He owned hundreds of treasure houses, bursting with gold and silver and precious jewels, but what the emperor prized most of all was his daughter.

The emperor loved his intelligent, kind, beautiful daughter with all his heart. Over the years, many lords and princes came from far and wide to seek the princess's hand in marriage. The emperor sent them all away.

"Not one of these ordinary men is good enough for my daughter!" he sneered.

One day, the emperor noticed a common servant gazing at his daughter with love in his eyes.

"How dare you look on the royal princess in such a way!" he thundered at the startled man, whose name was Wu. "Leave the palace immediately and never come back! If you're not gone by the time I count to ten, I will cut off your head! One . . . two . . . three . . . "

As the emperor bellowed, the fearful Wu dashed from the room. The princess hung her head in sorrow. Little did her father know that she was just as in love with Wu as Wu was with her.

Wu fled to the mountains, where he found many other unhappy runaways hiding. They had no food or money and they were starving and miserable.

"We'll have to become bandits," Wu told them.

With Wu as their leader, the men began to steal from farms, villages, and travelers. Stories of the dangerous bandits spread far and wide, and Wu's men became the terror of the emperor's lands. The emperor was furious.

"I want Wu's head!" he roared. "The one who brings it to me will be given the hand of my beautiful daughter in marriage!"

Soon every man in the kingdom was looking for Wu. Meanwhile, the emperor grew worried about the princess. She spent all day in her bedchamber, refusing to eat or drink or even talk. The emperor went to see her.

"What's wrong, my darling?" he begged gently. The princess didn't answer. She just sat still and silent, gazing into the distance.

Three days passed and, to the emperor's great relief, the princess recovered.

One day, the emperor and the princess were sitting in the garden when they heard shouting at the palace gates. The emperor hurried to see what was going on.

He couldn't believe his eyes. A giant rainbow-colored dog was striding into the courtyard—and Wu's head was caught in the shaggy hair under the dog's drooling jaws! The amazed emperor beamed and began to dance for joy.

"I will reward this wonderful creature with the juiciest bones in the kingdom!" the emperor sang. "The dog will have maids to wait on him! He will be—"

"Wait!" interrupted the princess. "That's not the reward you promised."

"But my dear," protested the emperor, "you can't possibly marry a dog!"

"That's what you promised, and that's what I will do!" said the princess firmly.

"Very well, then," spluttered the astonished emperor. 'We'll have a marriage ceremony, if that's what you want. Of course you won't have to *live* with the dog afterward!"

The wedding took place the next day. At the end of the ceremony, everyone cheered for the strange couple— but their voices turned to gasps of horror. The dog picked up the princess between its teeth and tossed her onto its back. Then it galloped out of the palace and far away.

"My daughter!" roared the emperor. "Stop them!"

As the emperor's soldiers hurried out of the palace, a huge storm suddenly began. Rain crashed down, and in only a few minutes the huge dog's pawprints were washed away. There was no trace to follow, and the soldiers glumly returned to the palace.

"The princess is gone!" the emperor wailed. "The beast will surely eat her, and I will never see her again! The whole kingdom must mourn for twelve months. Forever afterward, this year will be remembered as the Year of the Dog."

The year passed . . . then two . . . then three . . . then fifty . . . and the sad emperor grew very old. One day, he was lying on his bed knowing that death was near, when the door to his chamber quietly opened. The emperor's heart began to race, and tears of joy poured from his eyes. The visitor was his long-lost daughter!

"Father," smiled the princess, kissing the emperor. "Remember Wu, the servant? I loved him dearly. When you banished him, I sent my spirit to find him. That is why I was in a trance for three days. My spirit helped Wu cut off his head and live on, transformed into a dog. Then he came to the palace to win my hand in marriage.

"We have lived happily together all this time in the mountains—until Wu died. Now I have come home. I have twelve wonderful children, and they have sent you this present...."

The princess put a stick of licorice into the emperor's mouth. As he chewed the enchanted sweet, he magically became young again. He threw his arms around his daughter.

"Wu gave up his head to marry you," the emperor wept. "He truly loved you. I am sorry for misjudging him. Welcome home." And the emperor and his daughter spent the rest of their lives happily together.

JOURNEY INTO THE UNDERWORLD

A long, long time ago, there lived a very holy monk who followed the teachings of Buddha. Buddha said that people who gave up earthly things would find true peace, so the monk lived a strict and simple life.

He ate just one handful of rice a day and drank one spoonful of water. He had only one plain robe to wear. The monk gave up his house and all his furniture. He even gave up sleeping! Each night, the monk sat bolt upright in a hard, wooden coffin, his eyes wide open. Everyone knew there must be something special about him.

The monk also believed Buddha's teaching that people didn't live just one life, but many. He believed that when someone died, their soul left their body and went down to the Underworld to be weighed and judged. If the soul was heavy, it meant that the person had done a lot of bad things. It was sent to one of many hells for terrible punishment before finally being allowed back to the upper world. If the soul was light, it meant that the person had been good and kind. These souls were able to go back to the upper world right away.

All souls who left the Underworld had to get on an enormous wheel. Here, each soul was given a new body, so it could live another life. Good souls were given the bodies of leaders and nobles. Punished souls were given the bodies of beggars and animals. Each soul then drank from a cup containing the Potion of Forgetting. As soon as they had taken one sip, they forgot all about their past lives. They remembered only the pain of the punishments they had received in the Underworld. This reminded them to try harder in their new lives, so that they might be rewarded with better bodies the next time around.

Finally it was the holy monk's turn to die and go to the Underworld. For some strange reason, the monk didn't leave his body behind. He took it with him!

The Underworld was bigger than the most enormous kingdom on Earth. Eerie corridors and gloomy caverns stretched away as far as the monk could see. Everywhere he looked, groups of sighing souls were being herded this way and that by bossy Underworld officials. The monk set off at once to find the wheel so he could get back to the world above.

As the monk began to push his way through the crowded passageways, all the Underworld officials turned their heads to stare at him in astonishment.

No soul still with a body had visited the Underworld before! They had no control over such a being!

The monk marched down corridor after corridor. He walked past hundreds of doors that led to courtrooms. He hurried by murky tunnels that led to different, dreadful hells. Finally, he reached the huge wheel where souls were departing in their new bodies. Suddenly one of the souls caught sight of the monk and recognized him.

"I remember you from the upper world!" she called. "Do you know that your mother's soul is here, suffering terrible torment?"

Before the horrified monk could ask where to find his mother, the soul had drunk the Potion of Forgetting and was gone. The monk stood still in shock. His mother had died several years ago. The monk had thought she had lived a good, kind life and would be reborn right away. Now he knew she had been in torment all this time! The outraged monk was determined to find his mother and demand that she be set free immediately.

Back up the dim paths went the monk, into the heart of the Underworld. First he tried the courtrooms. He went into one after another, shouting and thumping his fist on tables and slamming doors behind him. The stubborn officials wouldn't tell him anything.

Next, the monk went to the gateway of each hell and asked the jailers where his mother was. They refused to tell him, so the monk took a deep breath and went into the terrible punishment pits themselves, calling his mother's name.

There in the awful pits of hell the monk saw souls chained upside down and souls being eaten by beasts. He saw souls nailed to beds, burning in fires, and wallowing in swamps of despair. The monk made himself look at them all, but none was his mother.

The desperate monk realized that he would never find his mother on his own. The Underworld was far too huge. Somehow, he would have to force the officials into giving her up. Suddenly the monk had a brilliant idea. He held an enormous party for the souls of all the dead monks who were waiting for new bodies. Thousands came! The sound of all the souls talking and laughing and shouting was deafening.

The Underworld officials were furious. The monk had practically stirred up a riot in their own kingdom! They decided to set his mother free so they could stop him from making trouble. The monk's mother was only given the body of a dog—but the monk was happy. At least she was free from punishment.

"Now what about me?" the monk asked the Underworld officials. "I lived a holy life, I defeated death, I conquered the Underworld. What kind of new body are you going to give *me*?"

In fact, the Underworld officials didn't give the monk anything. The gods decided that the monk had become so powerful in the kingdom of the dead that he should stay there. They made him the ruler of the Underworld, in charge of the hundreds of courts and hells he had explored. After all his years of sitting in his coffin, the monk felt right at home!

THE RICE ROAD

There was once a Chinese merchant who had made a huge fortune. He loved to show off his wealth by having the biggest and best of everything. The merchant had an enormous house, full of hundreds of servants. He wore expensive clothes and collected priceless treasures. His garden was larger than a public park.

The ordinary people who lived nearby dreamed of being as rich as the merchant. Most of them worked on his farms for very low wages. The farm workers lived in rundown shacks and struggled to feed their families. All they ever ate was rice, and there was never enough of it. Often they couldn't afford any rice at all.

One year the merchant decided to hold the biggest and best birthday party anyone had ever seen. He had his house decorated from top to bottom with colored banners and lanterns. He hired musicians and acrobats and dragon dancers and arranged for top chefs to prepare a magnificent banquet.

The merchant thought that everything was ready, but when he looked outside, he yelped in horror.

31

The road leading to his house was rocky and full of bumps.

"That won't do at all!" the merchant bellowed to his servants. "I want these rocks removed immediately and the bumps leveled out!" The merchant suddenly had an idea and a huge grin spread across his face. "Cover the whole driveway with a thick layer of rice!" he ordered. "Then lay a red carpet on top. I want the smoothest of all walks for my guests!"

The merchant was extremely pleased with his idea. Any rich man could buy rice to eat, but only *he* was rich and powerful enough to make a road out of it!

When the rice road was finished, it was the talk of the whole region. Beggars came from miles around to stare hungrily at the carpet. The desperate men didn't dare take a single grain from underneath. They knew that the merchant would punish them severely if he found anyone stealing. The merchant had put two guards outside his door to stop any beggars from bothering guests at the party. He had even ordered the thugs to beat any beggar who took leftovers out of the trash.

Just before the party guests were about to arrive, the guards gave the house and garden one final check. They were astonished to find that a beggar had somehow crept past them into the kitchen.

"Please spare a few grains of rice," the beggar pleaded. "My wife and children have not eaten for days."

The two guards didn't bother to reply. They just dragged the frightened beggar to the door and hurled him into the dirt outside. They kicked and punched him until his body was lifeless and still.

"No one will miss a beggar," said one of the guards. "If we get rid of the body, no one will be any the wiser."

The guards bent down to heave the beggar's body onto their shoulders, but try as they might, they couldn't lift him. For such a thin, feeble-looking man he certainly was incredibly heavy!

"Here come the first guests," panted one of the guards, sweating with the effort. "We'll have to leave the body here for now." They hurried back to guard the door.

The first thing the guests did was to marvel at how smooth and soft the red carpet felt underfoot. The merchant was delighted. His rice road was a success! He couldn't wait to amaze his guests with his splendid feast. As soon as everyone had arrived, he clapped his hands for the banquet to be brought in.

But there was a nasty surprise in store for the merchant. As the guests dug into the enormous feast, the rice in their bowls turned into wriggling maggots!

The guests leaped to their feet, shrieking with disgust.

"A magic trick!" the enraged merchant thundered. "Who has done this?"

The two guards looked at each other nervously.

"Sir, earlier we had to throw out a troublesome beggar," they mumbled. "Perhaps he put a curse on you...."

The furious merchant left his guests spluttering and squealing and hurried outside. His face turned red with rage when he found that a group of villagers had already discovered the beggar's body. They had called the magistrate, who was now examining the body and reading a letter from one of his pockets.

"This man is dead," the magistrate announced to the merchant, "and you are responsible."

"He was only a beggar," the merchant shrugged.

"You are wrong," said the magistrate. "This letter says that the man is in fact one of the Eight Immortals!"

The merchant gasped in shock and fell to his knees. The Eight Immortals were humans who had lived such holy lives that they had become like gods.

"I didn't know!" the merchant wailed. "Forgive me!"

"I should really take your life in return—" the magistrate began sternly.

"I beg you to pardon me!" the desperate merchant cried.

"If you will only spare me, I promise to give all my wealth away to the poor—starting with the rice road!"

The magistrate smiled to himself. The Immortal's letter had said: *Spare this sinner's life, but punish him by making him a road sweeper.* It had said nothing about taking away the merchant's fortune. The merchant had promised to do that of his own free will.

When the police came to lift the Immortal, they found that his body was as light as a feather. And as soon as they placed him in his coffin, he vanished. The Immortal had gone straight back to Heaven to tell his seven friends all about the mean, cruel merchant....

THE UGLY ONE

Hundreds of years ago in China, there lived a poor man and his wife. The couple had never been able to afford to go to school, so they both worked as farm laborers. The man and his wife had the hardest, most unpleasant jobs in the field—and they earned hardly anything. At the end of each day, the couple were exhausted. Their bones ached as they staggered back to their humble home. Every night they ate the same thing—plain, boiled rice, with cabbage-leaf soup on special occasions.

"How different things would be if we could read and write!" the man would often sigh.

"We would be able to have good jobs, with plenty of money!" the woman would say dreamily.

The couple were overjoyed when the woman gave birth to their first child—a baby boy.

"We will make sure that life is very different for little Kui," they agreed (for that was what they called their son). "We will somehow find the money to send him to school. He will study hard and become smart and successful."

No one said anything to the delighted parents, but everyone thought Kui was an extremely ugly baby. The poor man and his wife didn't seem to notice. In fact, as the years passed, Kui grew more and more ugly, but the couple loved their son more and more.

The man and his wife took on second and even third jobs to save enough money to send Kui to school. Luckily, Kui rewarded his parents' hard work by showing a thirst for knowledge. Each day he studied until it was too dark to read. As soon as it was light again, he jumped out of bed and began reading once more.

Even though Kui became very smart, he never grew big-headed with all his knowledge.

"I hope that I will bring you happiness one day," he told his parents. "I am determined to do well on my exams and become a respected government official."

First, Kui passed the local exams . . . then the city exams . . . then the provincial exams. He did well in every single one. Eventually, Kui was ready for the most important tests of all: the imperial examinations.

Finally, the big day came. Kui's hand was shaking as he wrote out all his answers.

When the results were announced, no one was more amazed than Kui himself to find that he got the top mark!

Kui was officially the most intelligent person in all of China. Now he had to go to the imperial palace to be honored by the mighty emperor himself.

It was a dream come true for the amazed student. As Kui stood in the huge, golden throne room, waiting for the emperor, he bowed humbly—so low that his forehead touched the marble floor. He didn't dare glance up until His Imperial Highness commanded him to rise.

The moment that the emperor caught sight of Kui's face, he gave a gasp of horror.

"It can't be!" he bellowed. "There must be some mistake! Surely someone so ugly can't be the top student in my whole land!" The emperor shut his eyes in disgust. "Take this revolting person away at once! Get him out of my sight!"

Kui turned and ran out of the palace as fast as his stumpy legs would carry him. He was absolutely heartbroken. This was supposed to be the greatest day of his life—for his mother and father, too. Instead of making them proud, he had brought shame on them.

"I have failed my parents," Kui wept, all alone. "They would be better off without me and my ugliness!" Kui no longer wanted to live. In total despair, he hurled himself off some high cliffs into the ocean.

SMACK! Kui landed on the head of a giant turtle! Some people say that the gods sent the turtle on purpose. Others say that Kui's landing was just lucky. Whatever the reason, the giant turtle swam so hard and fast that he soared right out of the ocean and into the air. His powerful flippers didn't stop moving until he had carried Kui right up to Heaven itself.

There, the ugly genius was finally honored. Kui was made the god of examinations, assistant to the great god of literature, Wen Chang. It was Kui's job to choose which students received top marks in exams, while it was Wen Chang's job to help the students do their best.

Once, a smart student prayed to Wen Chang after making a terrible mess of a very important exam. Wen Chang took pity on the student and that very night sent him an extraordinary dream....

In his dream, the student saw Wen Chang standing in his room and feeding all the answer sheets into a huge fire. When the papers had burned away, Wen Chang scooped up the ashes and squeezed them together. When the god opened his hands, he was holding a completed exam paper made up of all the very best answers. He handed it to the student, who read it excitedly and memorized every word.

Next morning, the student was woken by his friend banging on the door.

"Wake up! I have bad news!" the friend shouted.

"What's the matter?" yawned the sleepy student.

"There was a fire at the school last night and all our exam papers burned away," the friend explained miserably. "We're going to have to take the exam again!"

Of course, the student grinned from ear to ear. He could remember every single answer on Wen Chang's perfect answer sheet. And when the student retook the exam, Kui the ugly one gave him top marks!

THE ADVENTURES OF MONKEY

Since the beginning of the world, a large stone egg rested on the shores of the eastern sea. The egg lay there for thousands of years. One day it suddenly cracked and split open. Out jumped Monkey!

The delighted creature looked around and grinned. At last he was alive and free! Laughing and chattering, Monkey ran away to explore.

In the mountains, Monkey was overjoyed to discover a whole race of animals who looked just like him. These other monkeys were clever and cunning, just like him, but Monkey was by far the most clever and cunning of all. He soon became king of the monkeys.

Monkey ruled his kingdom happily for years and years until, one day, a worrying thought struck him.

"I cannot go on forever," Monkey said to himself. "What will my monkeys do when I die?"

All at once, Monkey remembered stories of a holy leader called Buddha. Monkey had heard that Buddha's teachings were strict and difficult to follow—but those who were successful were able to live forever!

"That's the answer!" cried Monkey in excitement and hurried into the world of humans to find a teacher.

The determined Monkey was a fast learner. After a couple of years, he knew how to turn himself into anything he wanted. After a few more years, he could fly through the sky on a cloud. At last, after several more years, Monkey was sure he had found the way to live forever.

By the time Monkey returned to his mountain kingdom, he had grown extremely bold and crafty from all his new knowledge. No one was a match for his magic. Monkey managed to kill a terrible monster—and its whole army too. He even stole a special weapon from the dragon king of the eastern sea. This weapon was a tall, iron pillar that could magically change into a deadly fighting stick. Monkey thought that this would be a very useful weapon indeed. He turned it into a tiny needle and kept it behind his ear—in case of emergencies.

In Heaven, the gods were nervous about such a mischievous creature having such strong powers. The Jade Emperor decided that Monkey would have to be controlled once and for all. He knew that Monkey desperately wanted to be important, so he came up with a plan.

"Monkey, you are so powerful that I want you to come and live in Heaven," the Jade Emperor announced.

"I am going to give you the job of Keeper of the Heavenly Horse."

Monkey was delighted. This sounded like a very important job indeed – but he soon realized it was all a trick. The job of Keeper of the Heavenly Horse wasn't important at all. Monkey was little more than a stable boy. The Jade Emperor only wanted Monkey in Heaven to keep an eye on him.

"Give me a truly important job," Monkey raged, "or I will make all kinds of mischief!"

"Very well," the Jade Emperor sighed. "You can be Guardian of the Garden of Immortal Peaches."

"That's more like it!" grinned Monkey.

For a few days he took great pride in his important new position, but soon he couldn't resist nibbling at the juicy, golden peaches. Before Monkey knew it, he had munched his way through all of them. They weren't ordinary peaches, either. The fruits gave the gods eternal life—and they only ripened every six thousand years!

Monkey giggled nervously when he realized what he had done. He definitely had the gift of eternal life *now*, but the fury of the Jade Emperor would be terrible!

Monkey fled in secret back to his mountain kingdom, but there was no hiding place from the gods.

The Jade Emperor soon found out where Monkey was and dragged him back to Heaven for punishment.

The Jade Emperor flung Monkey into a fiery furnace. He knew he couldn't kill Monkey, but he thought that the fire would melt him into many pieces. After forty-nine days the Jade Emperor opened the door of the furnace. To his amazement, Monkey jumped out, whole.

"Smoky in there, isn't it?" Monkey grinned.

The Jade Emperor was desperate. He threw Monkey into the hand of mighty Buddha himself. Monkey trembled as he waited for Buddha to squash him, but Buddha just spoke, softly and gently.

"If you can jump out of my hand, Monkey," said Buddha, "I will make you the ruler of Heaven. However, if you can't, you must return to Earth and work hard until you have made up for stealing the gift of eternal life."

"Fair enough," grinned Monkey. "No problem!"

With one huge jump, he leaped into the air. Down, down, down Monkey plummeted like a stone. Finally, after what seemed like hours of falling, Monkey tumbled to a stop. He found himself at the foot of five huge pillars that were so tall they disappeared into the clouds above. Monkey heard the sound of booming laughter around him.

"Sorry, Monkey," came Buddha's soft voice. "You haven't left my hand!"

Monkey jumped up and down with annoyance. He suddenly realized that the five huge pillars were actually Buddha's fingers. Monkey was still standing on the palm of Buddha's hand!

Monkey sighed a heavy sigh. He had been beaten at last. Now he had to begin a lifetime of work to make up for all his mischievous deeds. Monkey trudged away with a heavy heart. Little did he know he was about to have many great adventures! To this day in China, people still remember the cheeky hero and love to tell his story....

INDEX